Garan Holcombe

Super Grammar

Practice Book Level 6

CAMBRIDGE
UNIVERSITY PRESS

Contents

Present perfect with already/yet revision

Mustafa has already done his History and Geography homework, but he hasn't done his Science project yet.

Super Grammar

Use **present perfect** with *already* to talk about actions which have happened before now. *Already* means 'before now' or 'before this time'.

This is the form of the sentence: *has/have + already + past participle*

*Selma has **already** learnt to speak three languages.*
*Sophia is only 12, but she has **already** lived in Istanbul, Madrid, Beijing and Paris.*

Already is also used to say to express surprise that something has happened sooner than expected.

*Becky is only 12, but she has **already** learnt to play the violin, piano, guitar and trumpet.*

Use **present perfect** with *yet* to talk about actions which haven't happened up to now. *Yet* means 'up to now' or 'up to this moment in time'. We often use it to talk about something we haven't done but expect to do.

This is the form of the sentence: *hasn't/haven't + past participle + yet*

*Have you played on the new tennis courts **yet**?*
*Yes, I have. But I **haven't played** on the new basketball courts **yet**.*

1 Write the past participles.

1	become	*became*	5	send	
2	begin		6	meet	
3	catch		7	understand	
4	get		8	win	

2 Complete the questions with the verbs from the box in the correct form.

see ~~have~~ be fix finish call

1 Have you ___had___ lunch yet?
2 Have you _____ your homework yet?
3 Has Dad _____ my bike yet?
4 Have you _____ your grandmother yet?
5 Have your friends _____ the new *Superman* film yet?
6 Have you _____ to the supermarket yet?

3 Correct the sentences.

1 Have you tidies your room yet?
 Have you tidied your room yet?

2 Marco has already score ten goals for the team this year.

_____

3 I yet haven't had my lunch.

_____

4 We hasn't been to the new museum yet.

_____

5 I have had something already to eat.

_____

6 Paula have already finished her English project.

_____

4 Make sentences in the present perfect using *yet*, *already* and the verbs from the box.

learn be try visit read ~~do~~ see play

1 *I haven't done my homework yet.*
2 _____
3 _____
4 _____
5 _____
6 _____
7 _____
8 _____

who/which/where revision

This is the shop where I bought my trainers for gym.

OFALAND

PLANET SPOR

Super Grammar

Who/which/where are relative pronouns. Use these words to give more information about a person (*who*), thing (*which*) or place (*where*).

*Frank is the boy **who** won the school's painting competition.*
*Football is the sport **which** I enjoy the most.*
*Izmir is the city **where** my friend Ecem was born.*

1 **Complete the sentences with *who*, *which* or *where*.**

1   The city __which__ I like the best is Madrid.
2   My sister is the person _____ has taught me the most.
3   The place _____ I am happiest is my bedroom.
4   The thing _____ I like the most is my snowboard.
5   The sport _____ I play all the time is basketball.
6   The people _____ I love the most are my parents and my brother.
7   The films _____ I enjoy the most are full of action and adventure.
8   The hospital _____ I was born is very near my house.

2 Order the words to complete the sentences.

1 the / never / watch / sport / I / which / .
Tennis is _the sport which I never watch._

2 most / go / I / where / the / often / place / .
The school's Music room is _____

3 me / most / important / to / the / is / which / .
My bracelet is the thing _____

4 no one / except / the / where / can / go / me / room / .
My bedroom is _____

5 who / English / the student / best / speaks / the / .
Alberto is _____

3 Circle the correct relative pronoun.

1 The football pitch _____ we play all our matches is on the other side of town.
a which   b (where)

2 The girl _____ lives opposite us is from Barcelona.
a who   b where

3 The wood next to our house is the place _____ I take the dog for a walk.
a which   b where

4 Istanbul is the city _____ my uncle and aunt live.
a who   b where

5 The strawberry cake _____ my brother made for me was delicious.
a which   b who

6 The boy _____ joined our class last week is from Brazil.
a who   b which

4 Correct the sentences.

1 Yang is the boy where comes from Shanghai.
Yang is the boy who comes from Shanghai.

2 The park which we play is near my school.
_____

3 The motorbike who my sister bought is a Yamaha.
_____

4 History is the subject where I enjoy the most.
_____

5 Marta and Alba are the people where I like to be with all the time.
_____

Reading: a school newsletter

1 Read the newsletter. Write *True* or *False*. Correct the false sentences.

THE ALAN TURING HIGH SCHOOL NEWSLETTER

BIG CHANGES FOR NEXT YEAR!

FOOTBALL, BIKES AND RUNNING

Many things will be different at school next year. Students who love playing football will really enjoy our amazing new pitch, while those of you who want to join the running club will enjoy the new track we have already put in. We've also got lots of extra bike racks where the old Science room used to be and we would really like to see more of you cycling to school next term.

THE RAILINGS

We haven't repaired the railings at the entrance which were damaged in the storms last winter yet, but you should find that everything looks bright and clean ready for the start of the new term.

SAVED BY THE NEW BELL!

Our old school bell was not very popular.

Almost every day someone said, 'It's too noisy.' For that reason we have a new bell which we will test on the first morning to make sure everyone knows the new sound.

ANYONE FOR TENNIS?

We are delighted to welcome Miss Kulin to the school. She will be our first tennis coach. Miss Kulin is an ex-professional tennis player who played for five years on the tour. She will run the after-school tennis club three nights a week.

1 The school has got a new football pitch.   *True*
2 There aren't any new bike racks at the school.
3 The school wants more students to use their bikes.
4 The railings haven't been fixed yet.
5 Everyone liked the old school bell.
6 Miss Kulin has never played tennis professionally.

Writing

Help with Writing

School newsletters are usually sent out daily or weekly. They tell parents and students about competitions and prizes, new teachers, new facilities and future trips. Newsletters are written in a formal but friendly style.

1 **Complete the sentences with the words from the box.**

> teacher   trip   ~~changes~~   online   week

1   We would like to tell you about some big ___changes___ at the school.
2   We look forward to welcoming our new _____ .
3   We've had a wonderful _____ at the school.
4   We hope all our students will enjoy the skiing _____ at the weekend.
5   Students who want to join the running club can sign up _____ .

2 **You are the principal of Valley High School. There are some changes you would like to tell the parents about in the latest newsletter. Use the Reading page and the sentences in Exercise 1 to help you write your newsletter. Include information about the following:**

- Teachers (name, the subject the person teaches)
- Facilities (e.g. bike racks, basketball hoops, running track)
- After-school clubs (e.g. tennis club, running club, football club)

1 Present perfect with for and *since*

Inma and Alvaro have been friends since they were three years old.

Super Grammar

Use **present perfect** with *for* and *since* to talk about actions or states which began in the past and continue until the present.

Use *for* to talk about a period of time.

one day, two weeks, three months, four years
*Henry has lived in San Francisco **for** ten years.*

Use *since* to talk about a point in time.

last year, 2014, my birthday, this morning
*Katie has played the saxophone **since** the beginning of the year.*

1 **Write *for* or *since*.**

1	six weeks	*for*	6	five minutes	
2	last weekend		7	December	
3	this morning		8	last Friday	
4	two days		9	half an hour	
5	2015		10	eight months	

2 Circle the correct word.

1   Our school football team has won the league *for* / *since* the last three years.
2   My mother has been a clothes designer *for* / *since* 20 years.
3   My friend Sam has played the piano *for* / *since* he was five years old.
4   We've lived in this house *for* / *since* 2009.
5   My sister lived in Santiago de Chile *for* / *since* six months.
6   My brother has been interested in dinosaurs *for* / *since* he was a little boy.

3 Complete the text messages with *for* or *since*.

Hi, Alex. We've been here ¹ _for_ a week. It's great! I don't want to leave.

I want to be you! I've been in bed with a really bad cold ² _____ Monday.

Oh, no! I'm sorry to hear that. Get better soon. I probably shouldn't tell you – I've been on the beach ³ _____ we got here!

No, you shouldn't! Text me when you get home. You can come round to see my new phone. I've had it ⁴ _____ a week. It's got a great screen!

Lucky you! I'd love a new phone. I've had mine ⁵ _____ ages!

Yes, I know. You've had yours ⁶ _____ we were in our old school! I'm going to say goodbye now. I need to go back to sleep! Enjoy the rest of your holiday!

4 Complete the sentences with *for* or *since* and a time expression.

1   I've studied English _____.
2   I've lived in my house _____.
3   I've known my best friend _____.
4   I've been at my school _____.
5   I haven't tidied my room _____.
6   I haven't been away on holiday _____.

How long have you ...?

This hat is amazing! How long have you had it?

For a long time. My grandma gave it to me.

Super Grammar

Use **How long have you ...?** to ask about the length of time someone has been or done something.
How long have you had your motorbike?

In response to the question you can use either *for* or *since*.
*I've had my bike **for** five years* or *I've had my bike **since** 2011.*

1 **Correct the questions.**

1 How long have you speaking Chinese?

   How long have you spoken Chinese?

2 How longs have you lived in your flat?

3 Who long has your mother worked at the university?

4 How long has your brother be a police officer?

5 How long having you had a dog?

6 How long has you owned this piano?

2 Complete the questions with the verbs from the box in the correct form.

> study   live   have   know   ~~play~~   be (x2)   work

1 How long has your sister __played__ the guitar?
2 How long has your mother _____ a journalist?
3 How long have you _____ in your house?
4 How long have you _____ your tablet?
5 How long has your father _____ as a doctor?
6 How long has your brother _____ Anthony?
7 How long have you _____ Arabic?
8 How long have your grandparents _____ dance champions?

3 Match the questions from Exercise 2 to the answers a–h.

a For about two years. They dance every day! _____
b Since September. It's not easy to learn, but I'm enjoying it. _____
c For two months. She got a Fender for her birthday. __1__
d For a few days. I love it! It's much better than my laptop. _____
e Since she left university. _____
f For a long time. They met when they were about five years old. _____
g For almost 20 years. He loves his job. _____
h Since 2014. We love living here. _____

4 Write questions with *How long have/has you/he/she …?*

1 _How long have you known John?_____
I've known John since we were four years old.

2 _____
She's lived in Rome for two years.

3 _____
He's been a teacher for four years.

4 _____
I've lived in my house since I was three.

5 _____
He's played basketball since 2013.

6 _____
I've been here for 20 minutes.

Reading: an email to ask for information

1 Read the email and circle the correct words to complete the sentences.

fleurjack@treasureisland.com

Request for information

Dear Fleur Jack,

I am writing to ask you for some information about your Treasure Island Theme Park. I have written several emails before this one, but I haven't had a reply.

My friends and I have all been interested in pirates since we were young, and are very excited about exploring Treasure Island, especially about seeing the hammocks, treasure chests, palm trees and gold coins the photographs on your website show.

We have taken a good look at your website, but there are some questions that I couldn't find the answers to online. First of all, is there a discount for groups? There will be five of us on the day, two adults and three children. Secondly, are the rides safe for children of all ages? Finally, I couldn't see how close the train station was to the park. Is it a short walk or would we have to take a taxi?

By the way, how long has Treasure Island been open? A friend of mine says that the park has been open for two years. Is that true?

I look forward to hearing from you.

Best wishes,

Steven Robertson

1   Steven and his friends have been interested in pirates for *a long time* / *a few weeks*.
2   Steven *has written a few emails* / *has only written one email* to staff at the Treasure Island Theme Park.
3   Steven *has had* / *hasn't had* an email from Fleur.
4   Steven says that a group of *three* / *five* will go to the theme park.
5   Steven *doesn't ask* / *asks* about getting to the theme park.
6   Steven *doesn't know* / *knows* when the theme park opened.

Writing

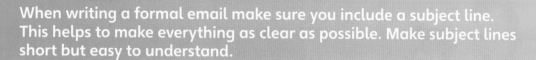

Help with Writing

When writing a formal email make sure you include a subject line. This helps to make everything as clear as possible. Make subject lines short but easy to understand.

1 Look at the email on the Reading page again. Complete the table with phrases used in formal emails.

A way of beginning an email	Dear
Explaining the reason for writing the email	
Changing the subject in an email	
Introducing points or questions	
A sentence to say you'd like a reply	
A phrase to end an email	

2 Write an email to Fleur Jack at the Treasure Island Theme Park. Use the phrases from Exercise 1. Include the following information:

- Say how long you have enjoyed pirate stories
- Ask how much the tickets are
- Ask how long the park is open
- Ask if there is a café

2 need to

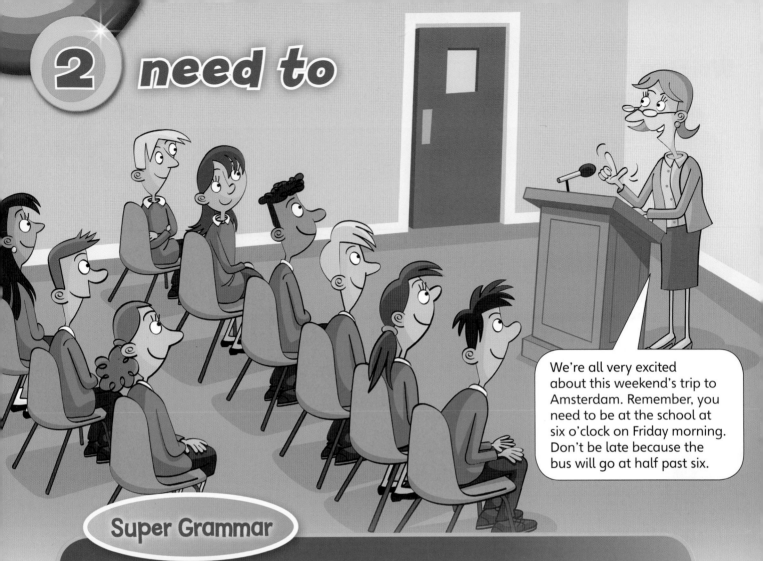

We're all very excited about this weekend's trip to Amsterdam. Remember, you need to be at the school at six o'clock on Friday morning. Don't be late because the bus will go at half past six.

Super Grammar

Use **need to** to talk about something that is necessary or an obligation.

*I **need to** study hard tonight. I've got a Science test tomorrow morning.*

Use the negative form, ***don't need to***, to say that something is not necessary or is not an obligation.

*You **don't need to** bring any food. We've already prepared an enormous picnic.*

---

1 **Complete the sentences with the verbs from the box.**

> ~~read~~ ~~work~~ exercise go practise get

1 You need to ___work___ hard to pass your exams.
2 You need to _practise_ every day to play a musical instrument well.
3 You need to ___go___ to university to be a doctor.
4 You need to ___get___ a good night's sleep to have lots of energy the next day.
5 You need to _exercise_ regularly to be strong and healthy.
6 You need to ___read___ a lot to increase your vocabulary.

2 Match 1–6 to a–f.

1 You don't need to tidy up.

2 You don't need to take a tent on the trip.

3 You don't need to catch the bus.

4 You don't need to tell Andy or Julia about the concert.

5 You don't need to bring anything.

6 You don't need to get up early.

a We've got everything we need for the picnic. _5_

b Mum will take you home. _3_

c I texted them earlier. _4_

d I'll do it later. _1_

e We're not going until after lunch. _6_

f They give you one at the campsite. _2_

3 Complete the sentences with *need to* or *don't need to*.

1 You _need to_ bring a coat, hat and scarf. It's going to be cold!

2 You _don't need to_ buy any milk. I got some this morning.

3 We _need to_ go or we'll miss the bus!

4 You _don't need to_ check the train times. I've already got them on my phone.

5 If you're going out, you _need to_ put suncream on. It's hot today.

6 We _don't need to_ buy tickets online. We can get them at the cinema.

7 I _need to_ call Grandad and wish him a 'happy birthday'.

8 Come on! We _need to_ score or we'll lose the match.

4 Write about what you need to do and don't need to do this week.

1 _I don't need to work this week. It's holiday._

2 _I need to study. I have an exam._

3 _____

4 _____

5 _____

will/won't

What will the future be like? I think there will be floating skateboards and jet packs!

Super Grammar

Use **will/won't** to make predictions (a prediction refers to something we think will happen in the future). After *will/won't* use the infinitive without *to*.

We **will travel** to other planets, *but we* **won't live** *on them.*

We often use the contracted form of *will* after pronouns:

I will	– I'll	it will	– it'll
you will	– you'll	we will	– we'll
he will	– he'll	you will	– you'll
she will	– she'll	they will	– they'll

<u>Yes/No question form</u>

Will we travel by jet pack one day?

Will there be food for all the world's people?

<u>Short answers</u>

Yes, we will. / No, we won't.

Yes, there will. / No, there won't.

<u>'Wh' question form</u>

What will the world be like in 3000?

I think it will be like a science-fiction film.

---

1 **Complete the sentences with the verbs from the box.**

> use   travel   work   stop   read   eat

1   How will we ___travel___ in 2050?
2   Will we __Stop__ using the internet one day?
3   We will __eat__ healthier food.
4   We won't __read__ books any more.
5   We won't __work__ in offices.
6   We will __use__ robots in our homes.

2 Rewrite the predictions using contractions.

1 You will go to Harvard University.
You'll go to Harvard University.

2 We will win the league next year.
We'll win the league next year.

3 They will make lots of money.

4 He will be a famous actor.

5 She will get all As in her exams.

6 I will climb Mount Everest.

3 Answer the questions with your own ideas, using short answers.

1 Will we travel to Mars? Yes, we'll.

2 Will we replace the internet with a new technology?

3 Will we stop eating meat?

4 Will there be more extreme weather like storms and floods?

5 Will people stop watching football? No, they won't

6 Will we be less interested in famous people?

4 Make your own predictions. Complete the sentences with *will* or *won't*.

1 There will be computers in tables, walls, trees and roads.

2 Most people will live until they are 150 years old.

3 We won't live on the moon.

4 There will be driverless cars.

5 China won't win the football World Cup.

6 People won't be happier.
will

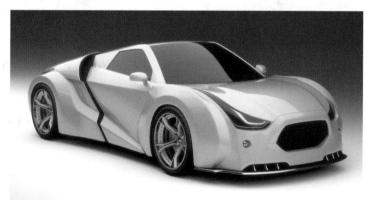

Reading: an advertisement

1 Read the advertisement and complete the table.

DRIVE THE FUTURE

Do you need a new car? Yes, you do! We **all** need something new once in a while. And the newest thing on the planet is our beautiful flying car – yes, that's right, the world's first flying car.

You won't believe how good it feels to fly a car. We know, we've tried it. Buy a **Zipwing+** today and this will be your future:

- You will avoid traffic jams.
- You will look down on the busy roads and smile.
- You will see our towns and cities from above.
- You will have the sky to yourself.

The **Zipwing+** has a solar-panel covering and comes with two top-of-the-range parachutes. Floating 10 metres above the ground, the **Zipwing+** can reach a maximum speed of 40 kilometres per hour and it will only get faster as we work hard on the latest designs and engines.

What are you waiting for? Come test fly one today. If you like what you see, the **Zipwing+** can be yours for a very special price – all that technology for only £500,000, down from the usual price of £750,000!

To book a test fly visit: www.zipwing+.com

Name of the car	The Zipwing+
What is different about the car	
How fast the car can go	
How much the car is	

Writing

Slogans are short phrases which usually go at the top of an advert.
The job of a slogan is to sell a product to someone by making an idea stay
in their mind. Slogans need to be short as well as interesting, funny or unusual.

1 **Match 1–5 to a–e to make slogans for adverts for cars.**

1	This is the	a	to see this car		___
2	Will you	b	drive the future?		___
3	You need to	c	car of the future.	1	
4	The future of the car is in	d	the air.		___
5	We need you	e	see this car to believe it.		___

2 **Write an advertisement for a car of the future. Include a slogan as well as the following information:**

- The name of the car
- What the car can do that is different
- How the buyer's life will be better with the car
- How much the car costs
- Where you can buy the car

③ Past passive

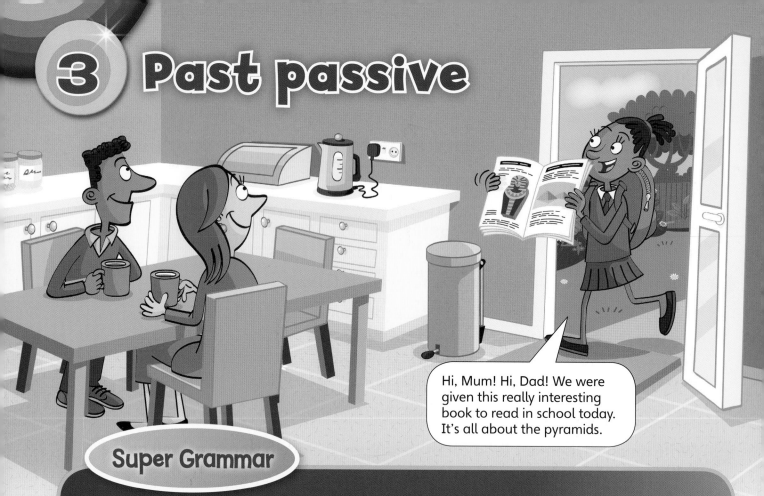

Hi, Mum! Hi, Dad! We were given this really interesting book to read in school today. It's all about the pyramids.

Super Grammar

We use a **passive sentence** when we are interested in who or what is affected by the action, not who or what does the action.

*This tower **was built** hundreds of years ago.*

We also use the passive when we do not know who did the action.

*The books **were stolen** yesterday afternoon.*

Form the **past passive** with *was/were/wasn't/weren't* + past participle. When we use a passive sentence but want to say who or what did the action we use the preposition *by*.

*The internet **was created** in the 20th century.*
*The first text message **was sent** by a software engineer called Neil Pepworth in 1992.*
*Don Quixote **wasn't written** by William Shakespeare, but by Miguel de Cervantes.*
*Pyramids **weren't built** in England, but they **were built** in Mexico.*

1 Complete the sentences with *was* or *were*.

1 The first email __was__ sent in 1971.

2 The first telephone call _____ made in 1876.

3 My laptop and smartphone _____ made in China.

4 The rulers of Ancient Egypt _____ called pharaohs.

5 The Eiffel Tower _____ built in Paris.

6 The museum in our town _____ visited by 10,000 people last year.

2 Circle the correct verbs to complete the dialogue.

Henry: Would you like to do this quiz?

Catherine: Go on, then.

Henry: All right. Don't look at the screen or you'll see the answers. First one. True or false: the modern Olympics ¹*was* / (*were*) started by Pierre de Coubertin.

Catherine: I know that one. It's true.

Henry: Correct! OK, next one – the pyramids were ²*built* / *build* by aliens.

Catherine: Oh, come on! That's not a real question. That's false!

Henry: Yes, you're right. Let's move on. Number three – the world wide web was ³*created* / *creates* by an American.

Catherine: Yes, I think that's true.

Henry: No, that's false. It was ⁴*invent* / *invented* by an Englishman. OK. The Surrealist painter, René Magritte, *was* / *were* born in France.

Catherine: That's false. Magritte was from Belgium.

Henry: That's right! OK. This is the last one. The 2014 Australian Open tennis tournament was ⁵*won* / *win* by Li Na.

Catherine: Oh, I've got no idea. I don't follow tennis … I'll say – true.

Henry: Yes! Well done, Catherine. You got four out of five.

3 Complete the sentences with the verbs from the box in the correct form.

> win   build   open   hold   ~~use~~   give

1   Paper was first ___used___ as money in China.
2   The 2016 Olympic Games were _____ in Brazil.
3   The Blue Mosque in Istanbul was _____ in the 16th century.
4   The Prado Museum in Madrid was _____ to the public in 1819.
5   The 2014 World Cup was _____ by Germany.
6   The Statue of Liberty was _____ to the USA by France.

4 Last night there was a break-in at the New Academy School. Make the sentences passive to describe what happened.

1   Someone broke the windows.   *The windows were broken.*
2   Someone stole the computers.   _____
3   Someone painted the walls yellow.   _____
4   Someone took all the sports equipment. _____
5   Someone moved all the desks.   _____
6   Someone threw rubbish in the playground. _____

a lot of / lots of / a few / a little

> We've got lots of olives but only a little cheese.

Super Grammar

Use **a lot of / lots of / a few / a little** to talk about the number of people or things.

Use **a lot of** or **lots of** when you want to say that there is a large number.

*There were **a lot of** people at my 12th birthday party.*

Use **a few** with countable nouns when you want to say that there is a small number.

*I got **a few** bananas from the shop.*

Use **a little** with uncountable nouns when you want to say that there is a small number.

*There's only **a little** water left.*

1 Write *a few* or *a little*.

1	_a little_ time	6	_____ dogs
2	_____ books	7	_____ fruit
3	_____ milk	8	_____ biscuits
4	_____ bread	9	_____ bottles
5	_____ eggs	10	_____ people

2 Circle the correct phrase.

1 There were a *lots of* / (lot of) people in the park.

2 I've got *a few* / *a little* DVDs.

3 There were *lots of* / *a few* cars in the car park – we couldn't find anywhere to park.

4 We had *a little* / *lots of* rain – the river flooded.

5 I only made *a lot of* / *a few* mistakes on my Spanish test – I managed to get 95%.

6 My parents have got *lots* / *a lot of* books – over 3,000.

3 Rewrite the sentences by changing the underlined words. Use *a lot of* / *lots of* / *a few* / *a little*.

1 There were only <u>six people</u> in the cinema.
   There were only a few people in the cinema.

2 We had <u>ten bottles of milk</u> in the fridge.

3 After I finished my homework, I had <u>ten minutes</u> to read before dinner.

4 There are <u>20 people</u> in our small swimming pool.

5 We've only got <u>three slices</u> of bread. That's not enough.

6 I only did <u>1 hour of work</u> this afternoon, then I went to the beach!

4 What have you got in your bedroom? Write sentences using *a lot of* / *lots of* / *a few* / *a little*.

1 *I've got lots of video games.*
2
3
4
5
6
7
8

Reading: an informal email

1 Read the email and answer the questions.

Hi Aunt Jane,

We're back from our holiday to Egypt. We had a really good time, but lots of things went wrong! First our flight was delayed. We had to stay at the airport for a few hours, waiting to get on the plane. When we finally arrived at our hotel, we weren't given a room with a sea view. The hotel was built 200 years ago and I wanted to tell the manager, 'you need to do some repairs,' but I didn't. Mum and Dad weren't very happy that our rooms weren't cleaned every morning.

Our hotel was near the beach, but there was a big storm the first day and the beach was closed – it was too dangerous to keep it open. We went to a museum instead and learnt about ancient Egyptian pharaohs, tombs and mummies. We bought lots of books on Egypt to take home with us. Unfortunately, I wasn't told that there was an exhibition on hieroglyphics until the museum was closing. We went back the next day, but the exhibition had finished!

The best day was the last day. We left Cairo and went to Giza, where we saw the Sphinx and the pyramids. There were lots of people there. Everyone took lots of photographs.

I hope all is well with you and Uncle Matthew.

Love, Amber

1	What happened at the airport?	_The flight was delayed._
2	How long did they have to wait for their plane at the airport?	
3	When was the hotel built?	
4	Why couldn't they go to the beach on the first day?	
5	Did Amber see the exhibition on hieroglyphics?	
6	What did they buy lots of at the museum?	
7	When did they see the Sphinx and the pyramids?	

Writing

The key to writing an email to friends or family members is to use a friendly, informal style. Use contractions (*I'm* instead of *I am*), use exclamations (!), and write as if you were talking to the person.

1 Complete the common phrases used to begin and end informal emails with the words from the box.

going ~~thanks~~ wait hope forward hear

1 ___Thanks___ for your email.

2 It's great to _____ from you.

3 How's it _____?

4 I can't _____ to see you.

5 I'm really looking _____ to seeing you.

6 _____ to hear from you soon.

2 Imagine you are Amber's aunt. You and Uncle Matthew had a day trip to London last Saturday. It didn't go very well. Read the information:

- You and Uncle Matthew decided to go to the Ancient Egypt exhibition at the British Museum.
- You went to London by train.
- The train was delayed.
- The exhibition was cancelled.
- On the way home, there were lots of people on the train and too few seats. You had to stand up.

Write an email in response to Amber's, and tell her all about your difficult day trip. Use the phrases from Exercise 1.

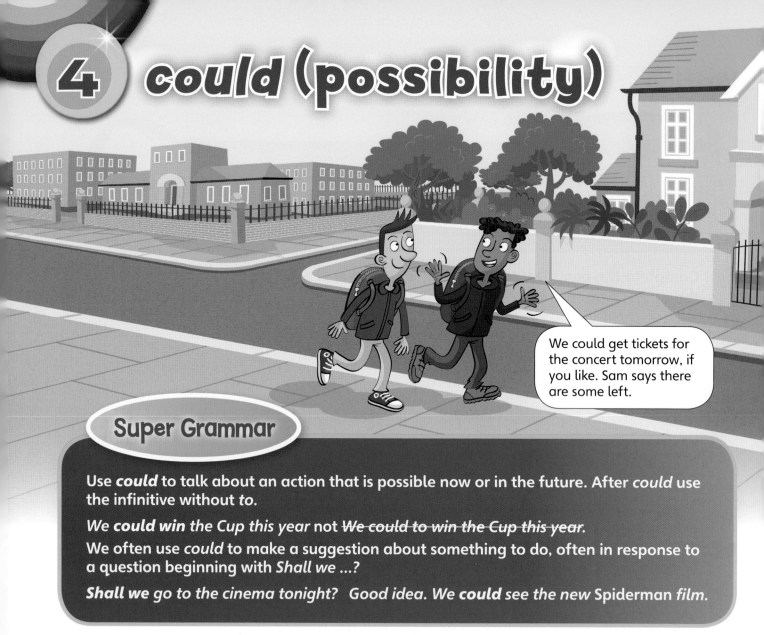

We could get tickets for the concert tomorrow, if you like. Sam says there are some left.

Super Grammar

Use **could** to talk about an action that is possible now or in the future. After **could** use the infinitive without *to*.

We **could win** the Cup this year not ~~We could to win the Cup this year~~.

We often use *could* to make a suggestion about something to do, often in response to a question beginning with *Shall we ...?*

Shall we go to the cinema tonight? Good idea. We **could** see the new Spiderman *film*.

---

1 **Are the sentences correct or incorrect? Correct the sentences you think are wrong.**

1 We could have chicken salad for dinner tonight.

Correct _____

2 We could go to see the match on Sunday.

_____

3 Jon's good at playing the guitar. He could joins a band one day.

_____

4 If we go to Bilbao, we could visiting the Guggenheim Museum.

_____

5 Sue's brilliant at basketball. She could play professionally.

_____

6 We could goes to the theatre this weekend. My sister is acting in a play!

_____

2 Complete the dialogues with the words from the box.

> go   watch   ideas   make   ~~shall~~   could

1

Harriet: What _____shall_____ we do tonight?

Anita: We could go to the cinema.

Harriet: I'm not keen, to be honest. There's nothing on.

2

Moshin: What do you want to do?

Daniel: We could _____ swimming.

Moshin: Great idea!

3

Toni: What shall we do?

Kate: We could _____ the football.

Toni: Oh, I think it's already started.

4

Cathy: What do you want to eat tonight?

Paul: We could _____ a pizza.

Cathy: OK! Let's go to the supermarket and get what we need.

5

Arturo: What shall we do on Saturday?

Bill: We _____ stay home and watch a DVD.

Arturo: All right. Do you have any good ones?

6

Alina: Any _____?

Bobby: We could watch the gymnastics on TV.

Alina: OK. I think it starts in ten minutes' time.

3 Write sentences with *could*.

1 Zack enjoys sport and watching TV. He _could watch the tennis._

2 Elizabeth's favourite things are exercising and seeing her friends. She _____.

3 Tomas likes meeting new people. He _____.

4 Mila is interested in painting. He _____.

5 Anna enjoys drinking coffee with friends. She _____.

6 Toby loves films. He _____.

Present continuous (future)

What are you doing tomorrow, Emily?

I'm meeting my sister for some cake at the new café by the cinema. What about you?

Super Grammar

Use the **present continuous** to talk about something we have arranged to do in the future.

We **aren't visiting** my grandparents on Saturday any more. **We're visiting** them on Sunday instead.

Although *going to* is also used to talk about personal plans, we usually use the present continuous when we want to be clear that a plan is definite – we know when and where something will take place.

When we say *I'm going to meet Jay this weekend* we suggest that the plan is not fixed yet.

When we say *I'm meeting Jay at three in the park* it is clear that we have arranged everything.

It is very common to ask someone about their plans by asking them the following question:

What are you doing tonight / tomorrow afternoon / on Saturday?

1 **Make sentences.**

1 I / meet / cousins / 10am.
    I'm meeting my cousins at 10am.

2 We / have / a picnic / on the beach.
    _____

3 I / see / Tom / at the concert.
    _____

4 She / play tennis / with Rebecca.
    _____

5 He / have / a party / for his 13th birthday.
    _____

6 We / fly back / on Monday morning.
    _____

2 Complete the dialogue with the verbs from the box in the present continuous form.

have   come   do   meet   watch   ~~play~~

Jim: What are you doing on Saturday, Will?

Will: My brother and I ¹ _are playing_ in a tennis tournament. What about you?

Jim: My grandparents ² _____ round. It's my mother's birthday. We ³ _____ a big party for her. It's going to be a surprise. Have you done the Science project yet?

Will: No, I haven't. I ⁴ _____ it on Sunday evening after dinner. Dad is going to help me. Have you done it?

Jim: Not yet. I ⁵ _____ Jen and Lucy on Sunday afternoon and we're going to do it together. What are you doing after school tonight?

Will: I ⁶ _____ the match on TV. Do you want to come round?

3 This is Lucas's diary. Write about his plans.

Monday
Meet Anne, 12pm

Tuesday
Basketball match, 3pm

Wednesday
DVD, Saul's house, 6pm

Thursday
Play chess with Mary at 10am

Friday
Swim with Mary and Saul, 11am

Saturday
Picnic, Mum and Dad, 12pm

1 On Monday afternoon
   he's meeting Anne.

2 On Tuesday afternoon
   _____

3 On Wednesday afternoon
   _____

4 On Thursday morning
   _____

5 On Friday morning
   _____

6 On Saturday afternoon
   _____

4 Answer the questions.

1 What are you doing on Friday evening?

_____

2 What are you doing on Saturday morning?

_____

3 What are you doing on Saturday afternoon?

_____

4 What are you doing on Sunday afternoon?

_____

Reading: a leaflet

1 Read the leaflet. Write *True* or *False*. Correct the false sentences.

The Olympic Sports Camp
at the fantastic Michael Johnson Sports Centre

1st July – 31st August
8:00am–5:00pm Monday to Friday

What are you doing this summer? Come along to our exciting Olympic Sports Camp! You could enjoy learning how to do:

Archery   Weightlifting   Fencing
Gymnastics   Boxing

This summer we are also offering a cool new class in how to prepare a healthy diet.

Ages 10–15

Cost £10 for a 4-hour class. Snacks, drinks and lunch are all included in the price.

Classes in the morning from 8–12
Classes in the afternoon from 1–5

All our brilliant sports trainers are fully qualified.
Sign up for sessions before 15th June to get a 20% discount.
For more information, call 612 333.

www.olympicsportscamp.co.uk

1 The camp offers training in six Olympic sports.
   False   _It offers training in five Olympic sports._

2 Last year's camp didn't have a healthy diet class.

3 If you are 12 years old you can go to the camp.

4 An all-day session costs £12.

5 You have to pay extra for lunch.

6 You can't get a discount after 15th June.

Writing

Help with Writing

Put what you want to advertise right at the top of the leaflet, use images, and make sure that you include contact details such as a phone number and email address.

1 **Make sentences with the words from the box.**

> information ~~fully qualified~~ learn included come discount brilliant class

1 Our trainers are ___fully qualified___ .
2 Sign up early to get a _____ .
3 Snacks and drinks are _____ in the price.
4 Come along to our _____ Summer Sports Camp.
5 You could _____ how to do all your favourite sports.
6 Please call for more _____ .
7 We're offering a great new _____ this year.
8 What's stopping you? _____ along this summer!

2 **Design a leaflet for a summer sports camp. Use the sentences from Exercise 1. Include the following information:**

- The name of the camp
- The sports people could try at the camp
- A new class you are offering this year
- How much the sessions cost
- How old people have to be to go to the camp

_____

_____

_____

_____

_____

_____

5 Present perfect with ever/never

Has anyone in the class ever been to London?

Super Grammar

Use the **present perfect** to talk about things that happened in the past at some time before the present moment. We do not say when the action happened.

*My sister **has lived** in Italy* not *My brother's lived in Italy three years ago*.

Form the present perfect with **has/have** + past participle. In informal spoken and written English we usually use the contracted form.

Full form	Contracted form
*He **has read** lots of books about London.*	*He**'s read** lots of books about London.*

Use the **present perfect** with *ever/never* to talk about things that you have/haven't done. *Ever* means 'at any time in your life up to now'. Questions beginning with *Have you ever ...?* are a common way of asking someone about the experiences they have had.

Have you ever met a famous person?   *Yes, I have. / No, I haven't.*

Never means 'not ever' or 'at no time in your life up to now'. Use the word with an affirmative rather than a negative verb.

*I've **never** met a famous person* not *I haven't never met a famous person*.

---

1 **Complete the sentences with *ever* or *never*.**

1 My brother has _____never_____ played the piano.

2 Have you _____ written a story?

3 You've _____ been to London? Really? I'm very surprised.

4 I've _____ been to Moscow, but I'd like to go there one day.

5 I've watched the *Star Wars* films many times, but my brother has _____ seen them.

6 Have you _____ tried Japanese food?

2 **Write the past participles.**

1 make __made__
2 see _____
3 swim _____
4 do _____
5 eat _____

6 ride _____
7 win _____
8 cook _____
9 build _____
10 buy _____

3 **Complete the questions with the verbs from Exercise 2.**

1 Have you ever __made__ a pancake?
2 Have any of your friends ever _____ a competition?
3 Have you ever _____ a tree house?
4 Has your sister ever _____ Polish food?
5 Have you ever _____ in the Pacific Ocean?
6 Have you ever _____ a horse?
7 Have you ever _____ a crossword puzzle?
8 Has your brother ever _____ a meal for the whole family?
9 Have you ever _____ a computer?
10 Have your parents ever _____ a film in English?

4 **Match the questions from Exercise 3 to the answers a–j.**

a No, I haven't. They're too expensive. _____
b Yes, he has. Many times. He's the chef of the family. _____
c Yes, I have. My brother and I did that with my dad when we were young. _____
d I'm not sure. I'll have to ask them. _____
e No, I haven't, but my mother has. She loves doing them. _____
f Yes, they have. They love watching films in other languages. _____
g No, I haven't. I think I'd fall off. _____
h Yes, I have. Once. Two summers ago. It was very warm. _____
i Yes, she has. She lives in Warsaw! _____
j Yes, I have. They are my favourite thing to make! __1__

Present perfect with simple past detail

Your mum's a great runner. Has she ever run a marathon?

Yes, she has. She did the Berlin marathon last year. In three hours and 42 minutes!

Super Grammar

We use the **present perfect** to talk about our experiences. We can begin a conversation about someone's experiences by asking them a present perfect question with *ever*.

*Have you **ever** tried snowboarding?*

We answer the question with *Yes, I have* or *No, I haven't*. If we want to tell someone more about our experience, we then use the **simple past**.

*Yes, I have! I **tried** it once, a long time ago, when I **was** on holiday in Canada.*

We can then ask further questions using the simple past.

Did you like it?   No, I didn't. I wasn't very good at it.
Where did you stay in Canada?   In Banff. In the Rocky Mountains. We really liked it there.

1. **Complete the table.**

Infinitive	Simple past	Past participle
drive	drove	driven
find		found
sing		
sleep	slept	
	broke	
drink		drunk

2 **Complete the dialogues with the verbs from Exercise 1.**

1 Have you ever ____sung____ a song in front of an audience?

Yes, I have. Last month, I _____ songs from *Les Miserables* to 300 people at my school.

2 Have you ever _____ tomato juice?

Yes, I have. I _____ some at my grandmother's birthday party. It was horrible!

3 Have you ever _____ outside?

Yes, I have. My sister and I _____ in a tent last summer when it was really hot.

4 Have you ever _____ across the USA in a Cadillac?

Yes, I have. My mum _____ my brother and me from LA to New York two years ago.

5 Have you ever _____ something valuable?

No, I haven't, but my friend _____ a gold watch on the street a few weeks ago.

6 Have your ever _____ your leg?

No, I haven't, but I _____ my left arm when I was six years old.

3 **Complete the questions with *has/have* and the verbs from the box.**

> be (x2)   read   live   upload   ~~see~~

1 ____Have____ you ever ____seen____ a play?
2 _____ your brother ever _____ to Guatemala?
3 _____ your mum ever _____ on TV?
4 _____ your sister ever _____ in another country?
5 _____ you ever _____ a video to the internet?
6 _____ your dad ever _____ a book in French?

4 **Match the questions from Exercise 3 with the answers a–f.**

a   Yes, he has. He read *Le Petit Prince*. _____

b   Yes, I have. Last year we saw a brilliant one about medieval London. ___1___

c   Yes, I have. Yesterday afternoon – it was my guide to learning the guitar. _____

d   No, she hasn't, but she would like to live in Australia. _____

e   No, she hasn't, but Dad was on the news once. _____

f   Yes, he has. He lived in Mexico for five years and travelled all around the Americas. _____

Reading: a book review

1 Read the review. Answer the questions.

A giant in Buckingham Palace *by Amanda Neil*

Roald Dahl

I have read many stories set in London – *Paddington Bear, Mary Poppins, Peter Pan*. I've even read Charles Dickens' *Oliver Twist*, as well as lots of his other tales of Victorian London with their strange and interesting characters going in and out of all the old shops of the city – the tailor's, the baker's, the jeweller's, the barber's. But the best book set in London that I have ever read is Roald Dahl's *The BFG*. I first read it when I was eight years old. I have enjoyed it several times since then; the last time was just the other day. Have you ever read it? No? What, never? Stop what you're doing and read it now!

The BFG was published in 1982 and has been popular with readers ever since. It tells the story of a character called The Big Friendly Giant (the BFG of the title) and the friendship that he has with an orphan girl called Sophie. Together, Sophie and the BFG have to stop the other giants, all of whom are horrible, from eating children. The pair end up going all the way to Buckingham Palace in London to get the Queen to help them.

What I most enjoy about this book is the language. The BFG uses funny, invented words such as 'snozzcumber', 'gobblefunking' and 'whizzpopping'. Dahl's character is like a perfect uncle or granddad, with a wonderful imagination, a big heart and a sense of adventure. I recommend *The BFG* to anyone who likes being silly with words and enjoys a good story, and especially, to those readers who want to be taken deep into the world of dreams.

---

1 Has the writer read any books by Charles Dickens?
  Yes, she has.

2 How many times has the writer read *The BFG*?

3 Who wrote *The BFG*?

4 When was *The BFG* published?

5 Name two characters from *The BFG*.

6 What aspect of the book does the writer like the most?

Writing

Help with Writing

When you write a review of a book, don't give away all the details of its plot. You should give a reader a sense of the story, not tell them everything that happens in it.

1 **Complete the text with the words from the box.**

> critics   recommendation   story   ~~reviews~~   opinion   information

Introduction to Book Reviewing

People who write book ¹____reviews____ are called reviewers or ²_____. A review has four main purposes: to give ³_____ about a book (the title, the name of the author); to describe the ⁴_____ (but not say exactly what happens); to give your ⁵_____ (if you think it is good or not); and to give a ⁶_____, for example, *You should read this book* or *I don't recommend this book*.

2 **Write a review of a book you have read recently. Include the following information:**

- The title of the book
- The author's name
- What the book is about
- What you think of the book
- Your recommendation

6 too many / not enough

> Oh, I've got too many homework exercises to do! I'll never finish them all.

Super Grammar

Use **too many / not enough** to talk about the amount of something.

Use *too many* to say that there is more of something than you need. Use *not enough* to say that there is not as much of something as you need.

*My brother's got **too many** video games. He doesn't have **enough** time to play them all.*

1 **Complete the sentences with *too*, *many* or *enough*.**

1 There were too ___ many ___ people on the bus. I had to stand up.

2 I didn't buy _____ milk when I went to the supermarket.

3 There are _____ many people on the London Underground.

4 Mum says she hasn't got _____ time to do everything.

5 I didn't have _____ money to buy the computer game.

6 I've got too _____ things to do today.

7 Dad's got too _____ CDs. They're all over the house!

8 My brother owns too _____ guitars. Last week he bought his fifth!

2 **Circle the correct phrase.**

1   (We haven't got enough) / We've got too many time! We'll never get to the train station by five o'clock.

2   There are too many / There aren't enough smartphones in the world. No one wants to talk any more, they just want to look at their screens.

3   She didn't have enough / She had too many coins with her. She couldn't afford to get a bottle of water from the machine.

4   There are too many / There aren't enough hours in the day! How can we get everything done?

5   We bought too many / We didn't buy enough potatoes. We don't need this many for a tortilla. Let's save some for tomorrow.

6   I've not got enough / I've got too many pairs of shoes. I don't need them all.

3 **Rewrite the sentences with *too many* or *not enough* and a suitable noun.**

1   We've only got two chairs. We need four.
    We haven't got enough chairs.

2   We've only got one loaf of bread. We need three.
    _____

3   We've got six big packets of crisps. We only need two.
    _____

4   We've got three chocolate cakes. We only need one.
    _____

5   We've only got one bottle of water. We need three.
    _____

6   We've got three packets of biscuits. We only need one.
    _____

4 **What have you got too many of or not enough of? Write sentences.**

1   _____
2   _____
3   _____
4   _____
5   _____

Can you tell me what this is for / does / is?

Can you tell me what this app is for?

It tells your TV to turn on.

Super Grammar

Use **Can you tell me what this is for / does / is?** to ask someone to explain the function of something.

Can you tell me what this button is for?

Questions beginning with **Can you tell me ...?** are a less direct and more polite way of asking someone something.

1 **Choose the correct words to complete the dialogues.**

1 Can you tell me what a screwdriver *do* / *is for*?
   It's for turning screws.

2 Can you tell me what *this is* / *is for*?
   It's a spanner. It's for holding and turning nuts.

3 Can you tell me what a drill is *for* / *this is*?
   It makes holes.

4 Can you tell me what this machine *does* / *do*?
   It makes yoghurt.

5 Can you tell me what a lever *this is* / *does*?
   It's a handle you move to operate a machine.

6 Can you tell me what a saw *for* / *is for*?
   It's for cutting wood.

2 **Complete the questions with the words from the box.**

tell   me   for   ~~you~~   does   is

1   Can ___you___ tell me what this is?
2   Can you tell me what this tool _____ for?
3   Can you tell me what this lever is _____ ?
4   Can you tell me what this machine _____ ?
5   Can you tell _____ what this switch is for?
6   Can you _____ me what this button is for?

3 **Match questions 1–6 in Exercise 2 to a–f.**

a   It's just a light switch. It's for turning the light on and off. Nothing special. _____
b   It's only a lever for starting that machine. _____
c   It translates things perfectly. It's a language machine. _____
d   This? No, I can't tell you anything about it. It's top secret. ___1___
e   This tool is very special. It's for, um – do you know, I can't remember. _____
f   Oh, this button is for increasing the temperature in the building. _____

4 **Complete the questions. Use *do*, *does* or *for*?**

1   Can you tell me what this is ___for___ ? It's for making bread.
2   Can you tell me what this machine is _____ ? It's for heating liquids.
3   Can you tell me what this machine _____ ? It cleans tools.
4   Can you tell me what these machines _____ ? They regulate the temperature.
5   Can you tell me what this _____ ? It cuts cheese into blocks.
6   Can you tell me what this is _____ ? It's for keeping things clean.
7   Can you tell me what these _____ ? They hold everything in place.
8   Can you tell me what this is _____ ? It's for mixing chemicals.

Reading: a blog post

1 Read the blog post. Write *True* or *False*. Correct the false sentences.

MY BLOG WORLD

Welcome to My Blog World again. What I want to talk about today is time. I just haven't got enough of it. I'm sure you know what I mean. There are too many things to do, aren't there? Every day I spend ages answering my little sister's questions. 'Arthur,' she says, 'can you tell me what this lever is for? Can you tell me what this button does? Can you tell me what happens when you press this switch?' (Yes, I think she is going to be a scientist.) I want to say, 'Go away!', but I am not an unkind boy. After I have answered all of Beth's questions, I feel tired and need to sit down.

Beth is not the only reason I don't have enough time. School takes up too much of my day. I've got too many tests to do and not enough time to study for them all. Another thing – I love reading, but there are far too many books to read. I'm interested in everything, you see, especially how things are made. Every time I see an interesting new book I really want to read it. It could be about Albert Einstein's life, the greatest inventors of all time or the history of the aircraft engine, but my 'Books I Really Want To Read' list is getting longer and longer and I sometimes think that instead of reading any of these books all I will ever do is make a note of their titles.

What can I do? Mum always says, 'Arthur, you're writing far too many blog posts. You won't have enough time for your inventions. Perhaps you should stop writing them.' Hmmmm. Maybe she's right. She usually is. Then again, maybe what I actually need to do is invent some extra time – now that's an interesting idea!

1 Arthur finds the time to do everything he wants to do.

   False   *He hasn't got enough time to do everything he wants to do.*

2 Arthur's sister doesn't ask him any questions.

_____

3 Arthur doesn't say 'go away' to his sister.

_____

4 Arthur has got too many tests to do in school.

_____

5 Arthur doesn't have many interests.

_____

6 Arthur doesn't think his mother's idea is a good one.

_____

Writing

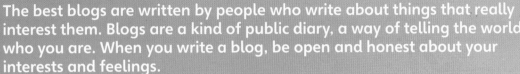

Help with Writing

The best blogs are written by people who write about things that really interest them. Blogs are a kind of public diary, a way of telling the world who you are. When you write a blog, be open and honest about your interests and feelings.

1 **Match 1–5 with a–e to make ways of beginning a blog post about time.**

1	What I want to	a	to talk about today.		_____
2	I'd like to	b	my mind today is time.		_____
3	The thing that is on	c	talk about today is time.		_1_
4	Today's post is all	d	about time.		_____
5	Time is what I want	e	talk about time.		_____

2 **Write a blog post about not having enough time to do things. Begin your blog post with one of the phrases from Exercise 1. Include the following information:**

- The name of your blog
- Why you don't have enough time (e.g. I've got too many things to do around the house)
- What you would like to change and how you would change it

7 Gerunds

It's true. Seeing the sunrise from space is an incredible experience.

Super Grammar

The **gerund** is the *ing* form of the verb. Use the gerund as a noun.

Learning languages is interesting.
I enjoy *learning* languages.

In general, to form a gerund, add *ing* to the infinitive: do   doing
If the verb ends in a single *e*, cut the *e* before writing *ing*:   have   having

Be is an exception. The gerund is *being* not ~~bing~~.

If the verb ends with a consonant–vowel–consonant
pattern, double the final consonant, then add *ing*:   sit   sitting

Don't double the letter *y*, for example, the gerund of *buy* is *buying* not ~~buyying~~.

---

1   **Order the words to make sentences.**

1   is / fun / cooking / good / .
    Cooking is good fun.

2   us / tired / makes / late / bed / going / to / .
_____

3   is / new / exciting / learning / things / .
_____

4   idea / every / a good / isn't / eating / day / chocolate / .
_____

5   your / dangerous / a helmet / riding / without / is / bike / .
_____

6   bad for / in / the feet / footwear / is / running / wrong / the / .
_____

2 **Write the gerunds.**

1 swim   _swimming_
2 live   _____
3 get   _____
4 travel   _____
5 study   _____
6 make   _____

7 come   _____
8 play   _____
9 go   _____
10 write   _____
11 see   _____
12 watch   _____

3 **Complete the sentences with gerunds from Exercise 2.**

1 _Swimming_ in the sea is more enjoyable than in a pool.
2 _____ to the cinema is always lots of fun.
3 _____ hard for exams can be difficult, but it's worth it.
4 _____ a good night's sleep is very important.
5 _____ friends in a new school isn't easy.
6 _____ the world by train, bus, boat and plane – that is my mother's dream.

4 **Complete the sentences with a gerund.**

1 _Doing_ homework is really boring.
2 _____ books is a great way to learn about the world.
3 _____ is my favourite thing to do. Sometimes my alarm clock doesn't wake me up!
4 _____ the guitar is my sister's favourite thing to do – she does it morning, noon and night. She's so noisy! She's quite good at it, though.
5 _____ on holiday is great fun. I love seeing new places and having a break from being at home and school.
6 _____ a foreign language is interesting, but it isn't easy. You have to practise a lot – speaking, reading, writing, listening. Everything!
7 _____ lots of time with my friends is very important to me.
8 _____ a big house isn't important in life.

Reported speech

Super Grammar

Use **reported speech** to tell someone what another person said.

*Chen said that **she came from Hong Kong**.*

In reported speech there are some changes to the grammar of the sentence. The basic idea is that what is in the present in direct speech, is in the past in reported speech.

Direct speech	Reported speech
I'm tired.	*My brother said that he was tired.*
I'm not going to the party.	*Mirko said that he wasn't going to the party.*

Notice how the pronouns and determiners change from direct to reported speech.

<u>You</u> have to study for <u>your</u> test.   *Mum said that <u>I</u> had to study for <u>my</u> test.*

The conjunction *that* is used in reported speech, but it can be left out.

Sally said that she passed all her exams or *Sally said she passed all her exams.*

---

1 **Complete the sentences with the verbs from the box in the correct from.**

> be   play   like   want   ~~listen~~   not want

1 He said that he ___listened___ to music every day.
2 We said we _____ the new English teacher.
3 She said that she _____ anything to drink because she wasn't thirsty.
4 They said that they _____ football in the park every Saturday morning.
5 You said you _____ to go to the cinema.
6 I said that I _____ from Russia.

2 **Circle the correct verbs.**

1   We need some milk.
    He said that they _____ some milk.   a needing   b (needed)

2   I don't enjoy watching sport on the TV.
    He said that he _____ watching sport on the TV.   a didn't enjoy   b hasn't enjoyed

3   I have to go to bed.
    He said that he _____ to go to bed.   a had   b having

4   We're going now.
    They said that they _____ now.   a went   b were going

5   I'm watching a film.
    She said that she _____ a film.   a was watching   b watched

6   This is a brilliant game.
    She said that it _____ a brilliant game. a was   b were

3 **Change the reported speech to direct speech.**

1   Millie said that she didn't like watching TV.
    I don't like watching TV.

2   Carl said that he was reading an interesting book.
    _____

3   Tanya said that she enjoyed writing stories.
    _____

4   Iain said that he wanted to go to the cinema.
    _____

5   Brigit said that she was from the USA.
    _____

4 **Change the direct speech to reported speech. Use** *that.*

1   I love video games.
    Martin said _that he loved video games._

2   I can't do the Maths homework.
    Robert said _____

3   My favourite food is spaghetti.
    Carly said _____

4   I'm having a great time!
    Lola said _____

5   I don't understand.
    Mia said _____

Reading: a travel diary

1 **Read the travel diary. Complete the table.**

The Diary of an Astronaut

Day 3

Space! I can't believe it. Here I am on the great mission – the Voyage to Mars. We're going to be on board a long, long time. We're all very excited. Jane Markham, our Commander, said that this was the best moment of her life. I agree. Being in space was my childhood dream – and now it's real!

Day 41

Everything takes so long in zero gravity! Going to the toilet – Ugh! Don't talk about it! But Samuel Conrad, who is our Chief Engineer, said that floating around inside the spaceship was great fun. He's right. It is!

Day 62

The food – hmmmm. It's like being stuck on an aeroplane. It's not great, but we're all getting used to it. The most important thing is to hold on to it or it will float away!

Day 171

Going into space must be very interesting, one of my fans said to me in an email. Yes, it is. I am a very lucky man. Alma Black (she is the youngest member of the crew, and our expert on the computer systems) said this morning that her life was like a science-fiction film.

Day 331

Looking back at Earth from space is an amazing thing to do. In fact, it is my favourite thing to do from space – our world looks so beautiful from up here. But I don't like the sunrises. We see them every 90 minutes – about 16 a day! I would rather see only one.

Day 427

Walking down the street, lying on my back in the garden on a sunny day, breathing fresh air – how I would love to do those things now that I can't do them! After more than a year on board, we're all beginning to want more room to move. There are 1,267 days left before we return home.

Name of the mission	Voyage to Mars
Number of astronauts on board	
Things the astronaut likes in space	
Things the astronaut doesn't like in space	
Things the astronaut misses about life on Earth	

Writing

1 **Answer the questions.**

1 What do you think the best thing about being in space would be?

2 What do you think the worst thing about being in space would be?

3 What do you think astronauts miss about life on Earth?

4 What do you think astronauts don't miss about life on Earth?

2 **Imagine you are an astronaut. You are on the first mission to Mars. Write a travel diary about your journey to the red planet. Include the following information:**

- What you do on the spaceship
- How you feel
- What you miss about life at home
- What you find most interesting about being in space

This isn't a very good film, is it?

Super Grammar

Use **question tags** with *be* to check information or to find out if the person we are speaking to agrees with us on something.

If the verb in the sentence is positive, the verb in the question tag is negative.

You're from Ankara, **aren't you**?

If the verb in the sentence is negative, the verb in the question tag is positive.

It's lovely weather, **isn't it**?

Put a comma before the question tag and use contractions with a negative form of *be*.

It's cold, **isn't it**? not *It's cold, is not it?*

1 **Complete the questions.**

1 The North Pole ___is___ one of the coldest places on Earth, isn't it?

2 Penguins _____ big, aren't they?

3 Female seals _____ bigger than male seals, are they?

4 A sledge _____ for sleeping on, is it?

5 He _____ knitting some mittens, isn't he?

6 Whales _____ mammals, aren't they?

2 Circle the correct answer.

1 Tom's a great swimmer, *is he / isn't he* ?

2 Burak isn't coming to watch the film about polar bears on Saturday, *isn't he / is he* ?

3 You're not reading that book about icebergs, *are you / aren't you* ?

4 It's hot today, *isn't it / is it* ?

5 You're interested in life in the Arctic, *are you / aren't you* ?

6 Your sister is good at Science, *isn't she / is she* ?

3 Use question tags to complete the sentences.

1 The Northern Lights are beautiful, __aren't they?__

2 Polar bears aren't black, _____

3 Igloos are made of ice, _____

4 The North Pole isn't colder than the South Pole, _____

5 You're drawing a picture of a seal, _____

6 Penguins aren't able to fly, _____

4 Correct the question tags.

1 The climate is changing in the Arctic, is it? __isn't it?__

2 Ice floes are sheets of floating ice, isn't they? _____

3 We're sailing to the North Pole, are they? _____

4 She's studying the Arctic, aren't she? _____

5 We aren't learning about glaciers today, aren't we? _____

6 He's watching a film about mammoths, is he? _____

7 You aren't interested in icebergs, aren't you? _____

8 Glaciers aren't getting smaller, are it? _____

may/might

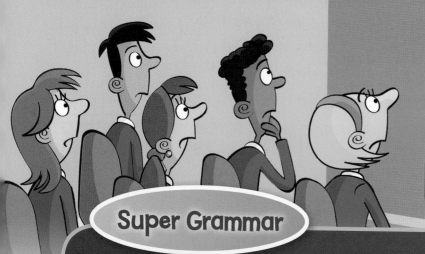

The weather might continue to change. We may get more storms. We may get hotter and wetter summers.

Super Grammar

Use **may/might** to talk about an action that is possible now or in the future.

*We **might** win this match.*

After *may* and *might* use the infinitive without *to*.

*We **may** go to Venice this summer* not ~~We may to go to Venice this summer~~.

May and *might* are often similar in use to *could*.

*It **may/might/could** rain later.*

However, notice the difference between them.

*We **could** watch the new* Ironman *film.*

(Watching the *Ironman* film is one of the many things that it is possible for us to do.)

*We **might** see the new* Spiderman *film.*

(It is possible but not certain that we will do it.)

---

1 Complete the sentences with the verbs from the box.

> start   have   go   want   be   ~~enter~~

1 I may not ___enter___ the chess tournament.
2 Miss Smith says we may _____ another History test next week.
3 Carrie says she may _____ writing a blog.
4 I may not _____ to the party tomorrow. I've got too much homework to do.
5 Andreas might not _____ to watch it. He doesn't like fantasy films.
6 It may _____ hot at the weekend. If it is, let's go to the beach.

2 **Match 1–6 to a–f.**

1 We may not play tennis this afternoon.
2 I might meet Julia tonight.
3 My friends may go to the beach on Sunday.
4 My sister might not go to university in the UK.
5 Our team might win this year.
6 It may snow at the weekend.

a That's what it said on the TV. _____
b I'll join them if I finish my English project. _____
c I think we're good enough. _____
d She may go somewhere in the USA instead. _____
e She's back from Galicia. _____
f Mum said it might rain. __1__

3 **Are the sentences correct or incorrect? Correct the sentences you think are wrong.**

1 It might be really cold at the weekend.
   _____Correct_____

2 Helen might not want anything to eat.
   _____

3 Sam says he may to come to the party on Saturday.
   _____

4 We may spend a week in Lisbon in the summer.
   _____

5 I might gone to the cinema tomorrow afternoon.
   _____

6 The polar ice caps might melting.
   _____

4 **Circle the correct verbs.**

1 My weather app says there _____ be a storm coming. Let's go inside!
   a (may)   b may not

2 Boris _____ come to the park on Sunday. His grandparents are visiting.
   a might not   b might

3 We _____ have a picnic tomorrow. Would you like to come?
   a may not   b may

4 Cristina might _____ some of her songs on YouTube.
   a puts   b put

5 We _____ go to the pool tomorrow. Everyone wants to go on the new slide!
   a might   b might not

6 Rana _____ know about the concert. Let's text him and tell him all about it!
   a might not   b might

Reading: a story

1 **Read the story and order the events.**

This Isn't A Story, Is it?

Yesterday was a most unusual day. Wherever Richard the Penguin went he was asked questions. He was cycling along an ice floe, on his way to his traditional Saturday-morning visit to the igloo library, when a seal shouted out, 'You're Richard, aren't you? My brother is in your How To Watch Out For Polar Bears class!'

Later, Richard was by himself at the library, and, as he was looking at the books about human beings and their ways, a seal pup appeared at his side. She said, 'You're quite tall, aren't you? Would you get *How To Fly* down from the top shelf?'

In the supermarket, where Richard went for some fish cereal, other penguins kept saying, 'It's hotter than normal today, isn't it?' or 'This weather is great, isn't it?' Richard didn't think it was great because he was very concerned about global warming, but he didn't say anything.

By the time Richard got home, he was wondering why people seemed so keen on asking him things. He had no idea. Just then, his dad came in from the large chunk of ice he had been sitting on, and said, 'Hi, Richard. You aren't hungry, are you? If you are, I'll make us some fish soup and we can chat about the day. Now, if you're lucky, I may have some prawns in here.' It was only when Richard was in his bedroom that night, and undressing before going to sleep, that he realised that the sentence on his T-shirt read, 'You're asking me a question, aren't you?'

a A seal pup asks Richard to help her.

b Richard's dad says he would make something to eat.

c Richard begins cycling to the library.   1

d Richard meets a seal.

e Richard goes to the supermarket.

f Richard sees the sentence on his T-shirt.

Writing

If the reader knows when a story took place, i.e. *yesterday, last week, many years ago*, it is easier for them to make sense of it. It is also a good idea to order the sequence of events in the story. You can do this by using time expressions such as *then, afterwards, after that, at that moment, suddenly, a moment later* and *later on*.

1 **Complete these sentences from the story with the phrases from the box. Then look back at the story to check your answers.**

> Richard was by himself at the library   his dad came in   Richard was in his bedroom
> that night   Richard got home   ~~was a most unusual day~~

1   Yesterday _was a most unusual day._
2   Later, _____
3   By the time _____
4   Just then, _____
5   It was only when _____

2 **You are going to write a short story about something unusual that happened at the North Pole. Use time expressions in your story. Before you write your story, plan it by making notes about the following:**

- The title of the story
- The plot (what happens in the story)
- The characters (the people or animals in the story)

If I could live anywhere in the world, I'd live in Egypt.

Super Grammar

Use the **2nd conditional** to talk about imagined events or states.
They can either be unlikely: **If I went** into space, **I would visit** the moon.
or impossible: **If I were** an animal, **I would be** a lion.
These sentences are formed in the following way:
If + past simple + **would** + infinitive without **to**
It is possible to say If I/he/she/it **were** ... or If I/he/she/it **was** ...

1 Circle the correct verb.

1 If I *meet* / *met* a famous person, I wouldn't take a photograph of them.

2 If I *could* / *can* go back in time, I'd visit Ancient Athens.

3 If I could fly, I'd *go* / *going* to the top of Mount Everest.

4 If I *had* / *have* time, I'd learn to play chess.

5 If we didn't have school tomorrow, I'd *went* / *go* snowboarding in the mountains.

6 If I were rich, I'd *gave* / *give* all my money away.

2 **Order the sentences to make a story.**

a   If I got really tired, I'd sit in my basket.   _____

b   If I fell asleep, I'd dream about chasing cats.   _____

c   If I ran around in parks all day, I'd get tired.   _____

d   If I woke up from my dream, I'd realise I wasn't a dog.   _____

e   If I were a dog, I'd run around in parks.   _____

f   If I were an animal, I'd be a dog.   __1__

g   If I sat in my basket, I'd fall asleep.   _____

3 **Complete the text with the verbs from the box in the correct form.**

> not be   read   can   not call   paint   not make   ~~play~~   not need
> remember   have

If, if, if … sometimes I think that 'if' is my favourite word. If I ¹ _played_ better, for example, I'd get in to the school football team. If I were taller, people ² _____ me 'shorty' and if I had a talent for painting, I ³ _____ my dreams. If I ⁴ _____ run fast, I would never miss the bus to school, and if I were good at Maths, I ⁵ _____ to ask Bonnie Mackintosh to help me. If I ⁶ _____ money, I would be able to buy that beautiful piano that's on display in the window of the music shop. If there were more time, I ⁷ _____ all the books I've got beside my bed, and if I had a really good memory, I ⁸ _____ everything I read instead of forgetting it all straight away. But I suppose there is another way of looking at all of this … If I ⁹ _____ sentences beginning with 'if' all the time, I ¹⁰ _____ me.

4 **Complete the sentences with your own ideas.**

1   If I could fly _____ .

2   If I could be anything _____ .

3   If I had a time machine _____ .

4   If I had all the money in the world _____ .

5   If I were a dinosaur _____ .

2nd conditional questions

What would you do if you were famous all over the world?

Super Grammar

Use **2nd conditional questions** to ask someone what they would do in unlikely or impossible situations.

What would you say if you met the President of the United States of America?

These questions are formed in the following way:

Question word (*what, who, where,* etc.) + *would* + infinitive without *to* + *if* + simple past

---

1 **Complete the questions with the verbs from the box in the correct form.**

> be ~~can~~ own live see have

1 What would you do if you ___could___ do any job?
2 What would you do if you _____ rich?
3 What would you do if you _____ in New York?
4 What would you do if you _____ four extra hours every day?
5 What would you do if you _____ a space rocket?
6 What would you do if you _____ a tiger in the street?

2 **Match the answers a–f to the questions from Exercise 1.**

a   I would give the money to people who need it.   _____

b   I would fly all the way to the moon.   _____

c   I'd make beautiful things out of wood and sell them for lots of money.   __1__

d   I'd climb a tree and then say, 'hello'.   _____

e   I would sleep.   _____

f   I would take photographs of the skyscrapers.   _____

3 **Complete the dialogue with the verbs from the box in the correct form.**

> meet   go   do   have   ask   be

Francois: Have you seen this website? There are lots and lots of questions – you know, what would you ¹ _do_ if ...?

Max: Ask me one.

Francois: What would you ² _____ if you could be anything?

Max: Easy. Footballer. They make so much money. What about you?

Francois: I'd be a painter, I think. OK. Another question – if you ³ _____ Lionel Messi, what would you say to him?

Max: I'd ask him if he thinks he is better than Ronaldo. What about you?

Francois: I don't think I'd like to meet him. All right – ready for another one?

Max: Go on.

Francois: Where would you ⁴ _____ , if you could live anywhere in the world?

Max: Hmmm ... that's an interesting one. I think I'd live in Vancouver.

Francois: OK, on we go. If you ⁵ _____ lots of money, what would you do with it?

Max: I think I'd invent a new kind of spaceship and travel to distant galaxies.

Francois: Last one – if you could ⁶ _____ me any question, what would you ask?

Max: When's lunch?

4 **Answer the questions.**

1   What would you do if you could have any job?

_____

2   What ability would you like to have if you could have any ability?

_____

3   Who would you meet if you could meet anyone?

_____

4   Where would you go if you could go anywhere?

_____

Reading: an online message board

1 Read the comments on the online forum and answer the questions.

DINO FORUM
where dinosaur fans talk dinosaurs

Discussion question: If you went back to the time of the dinosaurs, what would you do?

From: Fredthefossil Posted 4:12 pm

I'd get away as fast as my legs could carry me! I don't think our dinosaur friends would be interested in a chat!

From BrontySaurus Posted 4:13 pm

LOL! Great question. What would I do? I don't know! Take a photo from behind a big bush.

From MeRex Posted 4:18 pm

I'd jump into a swamp, throw stones at the dinosaurs and then go 'rahhhhhhh' to see if any of the creatures got scared and ran away.

From Jurassic Mark Posted 4:30 pm

Hey, MeRex. I've got another question for you – if one of the dinosaurs shouted 'rahhhhhhh' at you, what would you do? LMK.

From TheTerribleLizard Posted 5:00 pm

Can't wait to discuss the question, but I've got to have dinner now. BRB.

From HerbieVore Posted 5:01 pm

IMO, IRL, we would all be really scared and wouldn't know what to do. Imagine – no internet, no phones, no TV, and lots of huge dinosaurs running after us!

From PerryDactyl Posted 5:10 pm

Great question but can I ask a different one? Has anyone played Sunrise Horizon – it's a new dinosaur video game? LMK.

From Swampy Posted 6:33 pm

Hi, PerryDactyl. I have! It's brilliant! DM me and I'll send you a link to it.

1   Who says it would be very scary for everyone?   _HerbieVore_
2   Who can't answer the question because they have to eat something? _____
3   Who can help someone with information about a new game? _____
4   Who would shout at the dinosaurs? _____
5   Who has another question? _____ and _____
6   Who would run away? _____

Writing

Help with Writing

Abbreviations are a common feature of communication on the internet. It is a good idea to learn some in English that you can use if you chat to people on forums.

1 **Match the internet abbreviations 1–6 with the phrases a–f.**

1	LOL	a	be right back		____
2	LMK	b	in my opinion		____
3	IMO	c	laugh/laughing out loud		_1_
4	BRB	d	direct message		____
5	DM	e	in real life		____
6	IRL	f	let me know		____

2 **Choose a question to discuss:**

- If you were a dinosaur, which one would you be?
- If you could have a special power, which one would you choose?
- If you could fly, where would you go?

Write comments from people in response to the question. Include the following:

- A name for each contributor
- A time they posted their contribution
- A reason for each answer

Acknowledgements

The publishers would like to thank:

Design by Blooberry Design

The authors and publishers acknowledge the following sources of copyright material and are grateful for the permissions granted. While every effort has been made, it has not always been possible to identify the sources of all the material used, or to trace all copyright holders. If any omissions are brought to our notice, we will be happy to include the appropriate acknowledgements on reprinting and in the next update to the digital edition, as applicable.

Key: T = Top, B = Below.

p. 8 (T): BanksPhotos/GettyImages; p. 8 (B): db2stock/GettyImages; p. 19: ktsimage/iStock/GettyImages Plus/GettyImages; p. 26: exipreess/ iStock/Getty Images Plus/GettyImages; p. 32: Diane Collins and Jordan Hollender/Photodisc/GettyImages; p. 35: JackJelly/iStock/GettyImages Plus/GettyImages; p. 38: Tony Evans/Timelapse Library Ltd./Contributor/ Hulton Archive/GettyImages; p. 43: fotandy/iStock/GettyImages Plus/GettyImages; p. 47: Nadezhda1906/iStock/GettyImages Plus/ GettyImages; p. 50: World Perspectives/The Image Bank/GettyImages; p. 53: Danita Delimont/Gallo Images/GettyImages; p. 62: Feargus Cooney/Lonely Planet Images/GettyImages.

The publishers are grateful to the following illustrators:

Sam Church, Mark Duffin, Graham Kennedy, Alan Rowe, Simon Rumble (Beehive)